SO LYRIC IT FEELS SPIRITUAL

AN ANTHOLOGY OF BLACK WOMEN POETRY

EDITED BY
KIMBERLY F. MONROE

Unless otherwise indicated, all work is original from the authors in this book. All poetry and art is original and should not be duplicated.

Copyright © August 2017 by SAVANTS Publishing. All Rights Reserved.

ISBN-13 978-0692924242 (Savants-BAHP)

ISBN-10: 0692924248

All poetry is the author's and should not be duplicated in any form without the author's permission.

Book Cover Design by Christian Ryan West

Printed in the United States of America 2017

TABLE OF CONTENTS

EDITOR'S NOTE 6

KIMBERLY F. MONROE 11
   ROLLING HILLS 12
   LISTEN!!!!! 14
   GROWTH (gRōTH/) NOUN 15
   I KNOW A WOMAN (AN ODE TO BOBBIE MONROE) . 18
   MY "NIGGA" 20
   MFALME (SWAHILI FOR KING) 22
   A HI STORY 23

ARDELLA PLAYER 24
   CHAIR 25
   3 AM 27
   WHEN YOU MAKE HEAVEN ANGRY 28

KATRINA HARRIS 30
   HAVE YOU SEEN HER? 31
   SPROUT 34
   INDIRECT 36
   MEDIC 13 37
   THE UNTOUCHABLE 38

THE NEED TO PLEASE	39
SACRIFICE	40
ENERGY	42

DANIELLE SAVAGE 43

A LETTER FOR MY PRINCESS	44
A PSALM OF THANKS: PART I	46
AWAKE	47
DEAR WOMAN	49
FLUSTERED	51
FOREST SYMPHONY	53
HUMAN NATURE	54

BLYTHE DENNIS 55

FAIRYTALES	56
THE VISITOR	58

KOURTNEY THURMOND 60

I COLLECT QUOTES	61
GUMBO	62
HERSTORIAN	64
CHARRED STEEPLES	67
PASSIVE AGGRESSIVE SUB-POEM NUMBER 7	68
FLAMES OF THE PHOENIX	69
SLEEP TALKS	70
PRISMATIC LOVE	71

LANDIS ANDERSON 72
SISTERS 73
I KNOW A MAN 75
JUST THE TIP 79
YOU ARE TO ME 80
THE RAIN 81
DIFFERENT 82
EALY 84
MY BEST FRIEND 86

REGERNIQUE RASCO 87
HIGH 88
IF LOOKS COULD KILL 91
TRAYVON MARTIN 93

JA'MELL FAIRLEY 95
TELL EM SOMETHIN' 96

EDITOR'S NOTE

Sistren of the Quest

*"It's like the first day of school,
when the clothes is new,
the attitude is fresh
and we in the mood.
We keep it fresh and live when the vibe is high,
so lyrical, It feels spiritual..."*

Women's History Month stands out as a pivotal moment for the evolution of *So Lyrical, It Feels Spiritual*. In March 2017, I stumbled across the 1988 photo entitled, "Sistren: Black Women Writers at the Inauguration of Sister President Johnnetta B. Cole." Surrounding President Cole were influential Black women poets and academics like Bibi Nikki Giovanni, Bibi Sonia Sanchez, Bibi Gwendolyn Brooks. Bibi Toni Cade Bambara, Bibi Mari Evans, Bibi Paula Giddings, and others who have contributed greatly to the literature of Black women. For many young writers, these elder sisters continuously inspire our passion for poetry, activism, and scholarship. As prominent figures during Civil Rights and Black Arts Movements they have always expressed the good and bad conditions of Blacks throughout the African Diaspora. We are able to capture what it means to be Black women writers in America because of these giants. Asante! (Thank you!)

The photo made me think of Lyrical Quest (LQ) performing arts group at Grambling State University. Founded at GSU in 2008, the organization brought together poets, singers, musicians, and artists of all kinds once a week to perform. I've had the privilege of knowing all the women featured in the book during my tenure at GSU. I have memories and close relationships with each of them in different capacities since our college days. I connected with Kourtney Thurmond and suggested we publish a book of all the women poets from Lyrical Quest. She willingly agreed and we got started.

Taken from the Lyrical Quest theme song written by Deron Erthe St. James, *So Lyrical, It Feels Spiritual* is the most fitting title for the anthology. The lyrics represent a commonality of all the writers and how words are connected to who we are as spiritual beings. It reminds us of the importance of art, poetry, and music at Grambling. Where the culture of rap and trap music is becoming more popular, Lyrical Quest remains an outlet to those who still believe in real artistry. This work is a testament of how literature and poetry heals and breathes life into all things.

I will share my personal relationship with each writer in the order of how we met. Some, I met simultaneously, while others arrived at different moments. At whatever time they entered my life, they've all been a blessing to my growth and I've learned something from each of them.

As I listen to *The Heartbreak-EP* by Blythe Dennis, her voice is a reminder of great times at Grambling. Blythe and I joined LQ the same year. Having performed together many times, she stood out as a true singer and songwriter ready to spread her wings. As my first college roommate, I will always cherish the fun we had. The good food, music blasting, a few functions, and other craziness made my college days even better. Blythe's poetry is real and authentic, just as she is. Looking forward to her next project.

Landis Anderson and I met as Quest-mates. As a passionate and energetic poet, she releases some jewels to the project. Her humility is something I noticed very early on, in addition to her organizational skills. When she agreed to contribute to this anthology, I was reminded of all the good vibes of LQ rehearsals and performances.

Soulful Syndicate, a Christian poetry group, and LQ, are just a few of the spaces that connected Kourtney Thurmond and I. After she performed her poetry, I knew she needed to be a member of LQ. Her quirky attributes and dedication were only a few of the great qualities she brought to the table. I'll always remember our fun nights that involved writing poetry in hidden locations. The work she shares reminds us of life's small things that we often take for granted.

As members of the university choir and later Sigma Alpha Iota sisters, Ja' Mell Fairly became a pleasant spirit whenever she was around. I often felt that she had southern roots because of her hospitality; she always made sure her guests were good. The last few weeks she spent in Grambling were probably the most memorable. I remember attending her senior recital where she blew us all away with her performance. The poem she contributes represents her journey as a Christian woman.

I met Katrina "Kat" Harris in 2011 as a writer for *The Gramblinite,* the school newspaper. Our connection as friends was immediate, as we soon found out that we had a lot in common like being daughters of ministers. Since I've known her, she has proved to be outspoken and as a result, misunderstood. The work she contributes to the anthology is heartfelt, raw, and most likely brought tears to her eyes as she wrote it. Kat's work speaks to the heartbroken, strong-minded, and misunderstood.

In 2012, I was somehow the only woman in LQ and became known as "The First Lady of Quest," a role I was glad to bury when Ardella "Dee" Player became a member. Her poetry was deep and passionate. I remember thinking "Where did this serious sistah come from?" She always brought positive vibes and deep-thinking pieces wherever she performed. I was honored to attend her wedding in 2014 to support the union of Black love. Her pieces are the best combinations of imagery and play on words, beautiful.

Danielle Savage is simply amazing. She performed at LQ and around campus several times and killed it. I always thought she was a theater major because of the dramatic stage presence and voice inflection that had us following every word. Looking back at old photos, I remember when we opened up and had dinner with Nikki Giovanni. We then posed in a photo with Giovanni where she revealed her tattoo saying, "Thug Life." Danielle's poetry is a representation of her strength, womanhood, and spirituality.

Regernique Rasco and I connected on a trip to Europe. She was so down to earth and fearless that I was disappointed had never known her during our time in college. I remember her performing her poetry for talent shows and other events on campus. Truth is the only word I can use to describe the message she shares. The pieces she submitted represent the unjust treatment Black Americans have experienced for centuries.

My own poetry is a compilation of my life experiences and growth. There's always a sensitivity that arises when we share our personal testimonies with the world. My goal when writing is to be a voice for the voiceless and to find words to express fear. For some, poetry is an escape, for me it's an opportunity to renew, refresh, and restart. I left hurt, confusion, love, and other emotions on the pages with hope that it inspires all it reaches.

I would be remiss not to acknowledge and thank the beautiful beings that have supported this project since its inception. Dada yangu (my sister) Keli Monroe Wright has always provided positive upliftment in all my endeavors. You will forever be the epitome of what a sister should be. You taught me womanhood when I only knew sports and ponytails. The love I have for you is unmatched. Kaka yangu (my brother) Jared A. Monroe beat me up so much growing up that I feel like I can whip anyone. Thank you for always being an ear to listen and friend. It's no secret that you're the most talented artist that the world has yet to know. We'll be waiting.

Thank you to Christian Ryan West for designing the cover of the book. In my first book *Homecoming in Tigerland,* he did not disappoint. As a result, I knew I had to get him to design the anthology cover. Beautiful job once again.

My sister-friend Kourtney Thurmond was instrumental in reaching out to most of the writers featured in the work. I thank you for your patience and willingness to see the anthology come to fruition. This is only the beginning "To the Quest!"

I thank God for Gerald "Olufemi" Reed. Your encouragement, organic words, thoughts, and pesos were all God's timing. As you heard most of my frustrations to finish this project, you remained a patient, calm, genuine, and caring Man. I am blessed to have you in my life.

Asante to all the Black women poets that made *So Lyrical, It Feels Spiritual* possible. Your God given gifts deserve to be acknowledged far beyond your own notebooks. Thank you for believing in this project. It's been a pleasure, until next time.

Lastly, I would like to thank my parents, Pastor Abbie and Bobbie Monroe, for their trust in all of my dreams. It was my dad's typewriter and my mama's affirmation, "she's going to be a writer" that has gotten me this far. Thank you both for your laughs, acceptance, and agape love. My mama always says, "You can't choose your family." If I had a choice I would choose you both every time. I love you more than all the words in all the books in the entire world.

KIMBERLY F. MONROE

Kimberly "Zakiya Dada" Monroe is a two-time graduate of Grambling State University. Having received her B.A. in History and M.A. in Mass Communication and History in 2014, she is a Life Member of Grambling National Alumni Association who wrote the first children's book of GSU, *Homecoming in Tigerland*, as a way of giving back to her alma mater.

As a native of Lake Charles, Louisiana, Kimberly grew up using writing as a way to express herself. At Grambling, she was a part of various organizations, including Sigma Alpha Iota Music Fraternity, Lyrical Quest, and served as an editor for *The Gramblinite*— the school newspaper. In addition, in 2011 she founded Natural Sistahs, an organization promoting self-confidence for natural-haired women at GSU.

As a vocalist, author, and historian Kimberly never self-identified as a poet but always seemed to fall into the realm of writing and performing when she felt the urge. Kimberly is receiving her Ph.D. in African Diaspora History and Women's Studies at Howard University and her proposed graduation is 2019. She plans on being a History professor at an HBCU— hopefully Grambling! in 2017 Howard Graduate School awarded her "Most Likely to Publish Conscious Raising Books."

Kimberly Monroe

Rolling Hills

I never believed She had power
until she fooled you
Making you believe the bond was strong
like a 16-year-old skateboarder with a new shoe
She, tricked you
Make believe, play-friend, pretending
While my feelings shifted back and forth like a tire swing

I am forever changing
Never blaming my horoscope for giving me false hope
or compatibility stars,
I almost forgot who's in charge

She mastered,
Follow the Leader, Simon Says, Red Rover
and you came right over
The games were simple,
Like a domino ripple and you fell every time
Even "trump" could have fooled you

She rules,
Like a mighty tycoon
graced, only to be chased
so, get up out her face
if you're being replaced,

cuz She's quality,

no association with cowardly

only the common wealth of her country

which, is the body and She... is the caPitol city

Some call her Kitty-Kat with a "K" because She's sadity

Her strength failed at times...

Like when his body was fine

and her spirit was blind

only to find that satisfaction gave phony reaction

Emotion raging, Patiently waiting

Questioning my cognition,

failing to mention Her harmful ambition

But he was on a mission

Like a Jehovah Witness or better yet,

A politician knowing one lie would cost him the competition.

So, to be more specific... listen.

Black Women, my Queens, and my Soul Sistahs

Our Power will forever be questioned

So, let this be a lesson you can feel

There's Power in the Rolling Hills.

Kimberly Monroe

LISTEN!!!!!

To listen
Easy for some
A requirement for me
Sometimes I lose sight of that with
Distractions

Other appeasing gestures
My thoughts require not just an ear, but a brain
Not just a response, but understanding
 not just a person
But a listener.

Did you hear what I said?
Do I have to repeat myself?
For the third time!
Learn my language, the language of my heart, mind and soul.

Can you hear me now?
Call me back when you can.
The game and devices has your mind divisive.
And now I ain't got nothing to say.

Kimberly Monroe

Growth (grōTH/) *noun*

Why can't you just walk away?
It could all be so simple
If you leave things where you left it

There is no explanation or
Fancy remark, that can replace my feelings…
Let along my cold heart…

That beats for another
My King, who gives me enough attention
And more to spare but I don't like to share
And you would know that if you listened

Instead, you chose to diss them and kiss them
As if they deserve any part of the person I knew
For years
Where tears filled my eyelids
And fell on the floor that you walked on…

What is growth?

I thought that this time is the last time
I run back into your arms
where you held another
Or maybe this time you will stay

and not go this way or that way
And maybe this time, you will realize that I really loved you
And if words wasn't enough
my actions spoke novels.

What is growth?
When I finally gained the wisdom to walk away
You followed
Hoping to sabotage any relationship set for me
As if you were my Destiny

What is growth?

Growth is
hating someone
But having the wisdom to know that
Hate gives them power
So, I loathe you.

Growth is
Having the knowledge to accept every experience
Both positive and negative
As a lesson learned
So, I thank you.

Growth is
Understanding that you were just One man

And that there is a King set-aside for me
One that will appreciate every inch
And places you missed
So, I feel sorry for you.

After all, you are the reason
I know I deserve better
So, what is growth?
You're looking right at Her!

Kimberly Monroe

I Know A Woman (An Ode to Bobbie Monroe)

I know a woman who bakes red velvet cakes and sweet potato pies
I can't lie this lady is fly
Not because she raised five kids
But on June 14, 1988 there was no mistake
That she would guide me the next few years
To dry all my tears and secure all my fears

A bad bitch would be an understatement
But my mama is breathtaking
She stands 5'11, beat the shit out of breast cancer
And in the face of disappointment, she finds laughter

But her bare head made me embarrassed
And I missed every senior skip day
Because chemotherapy had its way

I know a wife of a preacher
Who finds joy as a teacher
Who taught me that not every man is worthy
She never questioned my spirituality
Because she knows I'm at peace with my reality
I know a woman who speaks words of Nikki Giovanni

Kimberly Monroe

and ends wars with words like Mahatma Gandhi

I know a woman who uses clichés and brainy quotes
Like "whatever floats your boat" and
"Cleanliness is next to Godliness"
I guess I get it from my mama then
So excuse my constant cockiness
But her voice has power
Like a combination of Nina, Billie, and Yolanda.

So whether I call her Mama, Ma Mere, Madre or my
Mother
She's my First Wonder
My Yeyo, Mrs. Bobbie Monroe
The woman that I know.

Kimberly Monroe

My "Nigga"

Yesterday I met a Nigga
Who said he didn't care
About his history
But it's his Story.

This Nigga rather believe a white man's lie,
Avoid reading it for his self he ignores it
And wonders why he lacks confidence

I said "my Nigga, this white man is inferior to you"
He knows that if you open a book
Your thinking would be so ingenious
because he knows that our ancestors built Egypt

But now he's just a
mis-educated, discriminated,
Christian-segregated
Nigga.

I yelled "Wake up my Nigga"
And to all who believed it changed
After the Emancipation Proclamation
Or that slavery is not a popular topic of conversation.
I'm sorry
But Drake, Lil' Wayne, Jay-Z or T-Pain

Kimberly Monroe

Won't give you the knowledge
To make A's in college
cuz simple arithmetic
is not longer the trick

my Nigga rather have a trick
than a lady, who's claiming it's his baby
he denies, the child support rise,
he calls her a Bitch…
homage to our lineage

I wish I met a Black Man
Who was enlightened
and not frightened to embrace his culture
But I met a Nigga.
Nothing more, nothing less
Just, a Nigga.

Kimberly Monroe

Mfalme (Swahili for King)

You are a Man!
From the taper fade
to your dreadlocks
As they interlock with my natural strands

Your intellect reflects my most inner belief
and when you blink
I realize that I, found actuality
As we share our spirituality
Our commonality is the bondage of our lineage

He speaks through his art
A poem, a song, his lyric makes my heart drop
My Black Brothah
With the Rolling of the Thunder
His sensual desire for the Black Woman
Is what my Sistahs need

And in case you've missed it
The Black Man has been Lifted
He's the epitome of Truth and
Living Proof that we
Cherish our Black roots
My Black Man
As you stand we honor your existence
And my people rise past steeples
And land in the Most High's Hands.
You are Mfalme!

Kimberly Monroe

A Hi Story

A Hi story that involves the ancestors
Grandfathers and music
Drums and harmonic infusions

A Hi school Story of ignoring
cuz I never really knew you
Until you revealed yourself to me
And now I see

My Hi college Story
Brings laughter and truths
While we're forever reminded
Of our pasts, the root

I was High off the first Hi
Ancestral links became minor
Yet, you're still here
And the rest is Hi-story

ARDELLA PLAYER

Ardella "Poetic Normandee" Player was born in Oakland, California and moved to Shreveport, Louisiana in 2007. She graduated from C.E Byrd High school in 2009 and later attended Grambling State University in the fall of 2010 up until 2012. Poetry has always been a part of her, as an outlet to expressing her inner self, but it wasn't until later on that she found more power in poetry and spoken word and really lived through her work.

Poetic Normandee found inspiration in the one thing everyone has in common and that was life and used that as a source for her work. Her hobbies include writing, painting, photography and makeup artistry. Currently, she is working as a Virtual Receptionist for a multitude of law firms and working to obtain a B.A in Psychology.

Ardella Player

Chair

White room, four walls

Front door, stairs

Emptiness, hollow halls

Four cabinets, all bare

Full roof, foundation

Front and back yards

Tainted windows, where the sun glares

Front door, back door

Both Hand rails

Living Room, Dining Room

Middle Floor, there is a chair

Cold, Lonely

Old oak wood

Few of its Kind, So rare

Abandoned, Mistreated

Along the body, kinks, nicks, and snares

Of all the things to leave behind, they leave me, a perfectly good chair

Generation of faces

Good people, good smiles,

And many new places

I'm a combination of all races

Engravings "Michael loves Brittney 1999", last of its traces

Loved, Embraced

Spring time, Room of flower filled vases

Ardella Player

Kitchen, Bedroom

Middle of the floor, there is a chair

The thrift store, goodwill

Other old chairs to compare

Tired, Exhausted

Right corner, was always there

Couch, Couch, Pillow tables carpets linens

All in pairs

Empty room, Locked doors

Wood has taken wear

Cold lonely

Old wood oak, few of its kind so rare

Abandon, mistreated

Along the body, kinks, nicks and snares

Of all the things to leave behind

They leave me

A perfectly

Good

Chair

3 AM

Here it is, 3 am
Where I'm positioned in my bed sitting up right casting my gaze outside my bedroom window,
Lost in the dead of night
With the exception of the twinkling of the stars and the moon, whom is in the process of making itself hidden behind trees to make rid of the emptiness of its absent audience
And despite all this, there I was
Awoken by my own metal patterns that projected themselves in my mind like a movie in my sleep
Playing back the hurtful memories that I still found myself draped over and unwilling to let go
Just yet
And I sit praying for a solution to the dilemma I am stuck with that countless shooting stars have been able to solve
And as I slowing comb the over the wound a hopeless arrow left behind with my finger
I am accompanied only by this same repetitive dream along with the different scenarios of what could be
And night after night
I sit
Awake at 3 am
Wondering if your finger in combing over your wound too

Ardella Player

When You Make Heaven Angry

Dear Heaven, I woke this morning with my good intentions bared on the sleeves of my night gown, bare to the moonlight. You shame me, you hate me, resentment fuels the wildfire in your eyes and my flesh burns like I am the woodlands animals exposed to your forest fire -Heaven I only ask you bear with me, be bear with me, and I won't be brief with you ill car for you, rescue me, save me like a stray dog with a homeless heart and I'll be loyal to you. Feed my soul and I promise I won't be anorexic to your superficial touch anymore and with open arms I'll give it my all like the 4th quarter game shot will make you proud

Dear Heaven tell me my late knocks aren't too late and won't go unheard. Whisper bedtime stories in my ear so I know your there as I drift off to our world take me from my disappointed expectations and sorrows, bleach my hands for temptation has a hell of a disguise and if you're not careful it will fool you.

Heaven splash sunshine sun rays across my canvas of oil pastels and spell out perfection in white ink. Can you pour your medicine into my cup so my health can restore I want to no longer see sickness when I look in the mirror? No longer cough or sneeze and not hear a bless you

Ardella Player

Dear Heaven present my flesh with a second chance so I won't feel it crawl anymore love me again like you did when days were warm and nights were young, like you did when Christmas felt like Christmas and the word family actually held meaning and didn't just spell out a word. Hold me in your warm embrace as this caged bird sings and I promise I sing you a symphony like I was all the instruments in the orchestra, and now when you hold out your hand I promise ill reach for it this time

And hopefully when you look at me I won't have to force a smile through my lips, no longer have to hold back tears from you, I'll no longer have to play "make believe" with happiness in front of you, no longer will the perfections of my imperfections perfectly engulf me Heaven undress me, I don't want to be shamed, hidden, covered. I don't want to struggle, drown, be held down earthbound, because with each breath me and gravity argues and with each exhale it wins, I don't want to lose anymore, be angry anymore, feel failure anymore

Dear Heaven, please tell me you're not displeased by me.

KATRINA HARRIS

Katrina "Kat" Harris is a preacher's daughter reared in the small town of Ruston, La. She attended Grambling State University from 2008 to 2016. Within that time period, she has earned 3 degrees, became fully certified to teach, joined Sigma Gamma Rho Sorority Inc., Sigma Alpha Iota Music Fraternity, and managed to become an award winning collegiate photojournalist as the photo editor of *The Gramblinite* newspaper. Before her love for photography, dressmaking, modeling, singing, and teaching there was her love for poetry.

Kat's poetry reflects times she has fallen in and out of love, moments of passion, and acts of desperation. She is inspired every day to not only make a mark but leave the lives she's touched with a feeling. There's something so pure and special about pen to paper. With mere words, you can create feelings and memories to last forever and that's just what she hopes to do with these works.

Katrina Harris

Have You Seen Her?...

Things weren't always this way with me
my mannerisms toward life were modest and sweet
I was happily bound in my trapped personality
content with loneliness, pity and mistreat.

Something began to tug at my feet
pulling me out of what comforted me
I heard its whispers in my days and screams in my nights
something was trying to take my life

I dreamed of darkness, shadows, and misery
Why was this entity troubling me?
Don't I have my life in control?
Something was trying to take my soul.

"You won't be respected until you put up a fight
you've got to break the rules to come out of strife
You don't have to be so modest to get where you need to be
If you do what I'll say then you will be free"

The voice was soft and convincing
yet filled with uncertainties
it was right, I can't get anywhere being modest and sweet
but isn't this the way to be?

Katrina Harris

Ill decline its offer and pray for peace

I heard it scream later on that night
Its voice was filled with anger and spite
"You're going to hand over your thoughts, actions, and emotion
you will become like slaves and freely submit your devotion"

The validity in this voice may be nonexistent to you,
but this evil commander felt real and true
I tried to fight its forceful grasps
but nothing would prepare me for its next task

It gained power by moonlight
and froze my body in time
I didn't wanna see, I was petrified
severely afraid of the horrors I would find

when I finally opened up my eyes
this entity rejoiced at my demise
it stared through my eyes like opened windows
and took my soul into the shadows

These days I find myself bitter and mean
Doing everything to be happy and free
I changed my hair, my friends, and my ways
Only to find inescapable dismay

Katrina Harris

Do you know what happened to me?
I can't find my way back to sanity
I just want to smile, laugh, and breathe
This is my sincerest desperate plea.

Katrina Harris

Sprout

Specifically designed

Planted in perfect timing

A host for the soul that I insisted to exist

Brought forth in reconciliation

But only through the life and death of my temptations

We called heaven

Hell came first

Trouble, agony, pain, and toil

Yet a balm was waiting in the rafters

to be planted in different soil

Something had to even the score

With equal agony must come equal joy

Heaven arrived just in time

It's song is sweet like the wind chime

A sprout, innocent and unknowing

To reconnect and heal the love that was not growing.

It took me a while to realize that the balm was not mine.

I was the host for a different Divine

A type of soul saving intervention

Something that may forever go unmentioned

My balm was different

Katrina Harris

It hurt like alcohol on an open wound
Cleaning out all of the negative energy
I had let in to me
My balm hurt, but brought me to joy
Despite the unfortunate intent to destroy

This phallus was like a two-edged sword
Working to bring me pain but give you a reward.

A reward of forever
And whether that forever be tormented
Unwarranted
It's yours

You're welcome
But, thank you

Enjoy

Katrina Harris

Indirect

Before forever keeps you occupied

I'd like a moment of your time

I'll touch your heart with my finger tip

and replace the beat that took your shine

I'll revive you

on purpose...for purpose

in love... for love....

and if the balm keeps you content

with lullabies and newborn scents…

I'd know the indirect effect of my electricity

incited the life that came to be

-KAT

Katrina Harris

Medic 13

I know you don't know me but
Can I ask you something
What was it? What caused you to save every life but mine

When you breathed life into my lungs
You gave up
You didn't bother to check my pulse
3 years I'd been working to stay alive
And you chose to take away that precious time

You explored every part of my anatomy
But didn't take the time to resuscitate me
You took care of my shivering body
But failed to restore my vitality

You told me I'd be fine and you were my forever fix
But can you tell me why your promises were filled with conflicts

You looked me right in my eyes as I lay on cold white sheets
Just to say you were giving up on me
There was another life that you wanted to revive
and it was well worth the loss of mine

Katrina Harris

The Untouchable....

I'll make a fool out of myself for it and ruin my reputation,
I'll stop what I'm doing just for its satisfaction,
I'll wake up in the middle of the night just to prove my good deeds
but when it's all said and done it never gives me what I need

I'm sure I've cried rivers for its disappointing times
I'm sure I can write a book of all its betraying lies
I'm sure I've lost a million friends from its misleading ways
but it just doesn't seem to care about the sacrifices I've made

I go in at it blind, cuz I trust what it does to me,
go in at it slow cuz I want it to last,
I dig down deep to get the real feel of its essence,
but just when I think I've reached my destination,
reality grabs me by my ankles and snatches me away from the... Untouchable [Love]

Katrina Harris

The Need to Please

Those words of deceit arouse me...the evils inside you hypnotize me, those eyes are filled with ill intentions and I love it, like a bug to a flame I am attracted to the burns of your guile, rip down my guard, touch me, stain my heart with your wicked cruelty, this urge takes control over my actions and I submit.

What is this force inside me that allows me to release my hold on reality, what draws me to love the iniquity that manifest inside mankind.

With every lie my back arches in pleasure, with every corrupt look my body explodes in desire, those words of deception drive me to my climax, the lack of affection makes me surge into ecstasy, then reality comes to steal my euphoria away, its hard blows hit my mind first and goes deeper to strike me in the heart and I love it I love it hard there is so much pleasure in its pain...the need to please.

Katrina Harris

Sacrifice

Freely, openly, abundantly
without restraint or limitations
to inhale and exhale its delicate breeze
I wanted to encode my DNA with this strange disease

I opened my pores
I wanted it to make my skin glow
just like my mothers after 40 years
I was adjusting my life because this felt real

I gave myself away
I became an honest sacrifice
to trade my mind body and spirit
Indeed....this was a fair price

My world stopped for it
In an attempt to win the war
I left my schedule unattended
just to admire and adore

It was happening to me
I was consumed by its works
I didn't want to belong to me again
I felt this is where my true existence began

I felt a peace over my mind

Katrina Harris

troubles were so far away

memories of the past that haunted me were fading

and all I wanted to do was obey

I was changed...It changed me

and Even though it was just for a little while

I held on as long as I could

Just to enjoy how it made me smile

Genuine, sincere, delicate, and real

I would sacrifice me just to experience how love feels

Katrina Harris

Energy

If the eyes are the windows to the soul then I've seen yours

silent, calmed, humbled but loud

So clearly it beaconed and resisted

all in the same breath

and that's when I knew...

I knew I could devour you

The purity in celibacy

allows one to hear the silent cries

of the passion deprived

and I hear you

oh, if I could only pacify

the needs that you and I

have acquired

you would hunger no more

but those stars don't align in this lifetime

DANIELLE SAVAGE

Danielle Savage is an Oakland, California native. She is a mommy, a school-teacher, and a lover of Christ. Danielle graduated from Grambling State University in 2012. She enjoys relaxing with her daughter, kicking it with her students, and hanging with her family.

Danielle Savage

A Letter for My Princess

Don't waste your time trying to be perfect.
Because no one is, slow down baby, it's going to be okay. Don't waste your time worrying about what others think of you, slow down, some things just happen that way.
You will have lessons learned, and you will have bridges burned. You will have people in your life that's gonna make your stomach turn.
But you know what, when you satisfy yourself first, well baby there is no greater feeling, when you put your needs and wants at the top of the list, you have just begun your healing.
Don't worry about these newscasters, these politicians trying to get us all into competition, these dollies on our radio stations corrupting our children. These jiggaboo puppets reinforcing everything that Masa' told us was, got brothers from the suburbs walking around banging like they thugs. But we all just want to feel love. To be joyous and to be content, to find a love that was heaven sent.
But child, ain't nobody gon' wanna be around you if your words are never meant. You don't have to dress yourself up to hide a smile that always bent, painting over instead of going under to find out the true hindrance. And you ain't always gotta be hard as cement, take five minutes to breathe baby, and find a

more positive way to vent. And when your friends they desert you, don't fret take a hint you're moving on to bigger magnitudes, just trust in Him.

This life is not easy and your tears don't make you weak, release, and reject what everybody told you to be. You are unique. Accept your inner power because your waters run deep!

And if he ain't trying to fool with you, cause you ain't no freak, let it ride. They always come back just make sure you don't back slide. Get out of that pride it will hurt you in the long run. Push fake friends aside, see me I'm bolo, and I'm on one. Still trying to find that <u>balance</u>. But I'd rather have the few and the loyal than the fake and the plentiful.

Envious hearts are <u>calloused</u>, plastering up heart aches only to leave them with cemented souls. But out of the concrete I rose and darling I just want you to do the same. Sometimes we make mistakes and fall, charge it to the game.

Cause there is one thing that will stick and will never cease to remain, and that's the He who lives in you, so when it's time to, don't be afraid to change.

Danielle Savage

A Psalm of Thanks: Part I

I smile because He loves me. So glad He gives me everything I need. In due time His greatness in the earth will be unfolded. For it's not about me.

Jesus.

What noble Big Brother is He? Died for me, cried for me, reigned for me, my peace.

Breath in my body, light in my eyes, it's Jesus.

Move Holy Spirit. My strength and my joy. Dwell right beside me. Whisper in my ear.

Poetry. Heavenly. sweet sounds of healing, love, and humility.

Pride-breaking, anger-changing, melodies from heaven. Contentment in every situation. Rain down on me.

 Still, calm, gentle waters. Serene. Heavenly characteristics. Peace.

To the Most High Living God be glory, power, honor, worship and praise.

Forever. Amen.

Danielle Savage

Awake

The more I learn the more I earn, these badges of heavy burden. I have no choice, but to be a voice for the truth and the people servant.

Dear Lord eliminate my doubts, for I know that they are plentiful. Illuminate my mouth for I want to be instrumental. If it is in Your will let me help the people build, letting the wisdom be their shield, I will cry from the top of the hills, "wake up, get motivated, you are subconsciously dying. Yearn for more learn from more than the feeble satisfaction of voting for your favorite villain".

Bone chilling, when you think of what aspects of our lives we are not in control of. We battle because of our differences causes are so materialistic. It's so easy to become pessimistic when you develop a conscious mind. And the ignorance is bliss as long as we make a conscious decision to stay blind.

Confined in our bubbles as our space gets tighter and tighter, squeezing our rights, squeezing the fight, as the idealistic black woman's skin tone becomes lighter and lighter. And we strive for what? So we can stunt on niggas in the 'jects? Get breaded up to look down on people who are still in the place that we just left. And then acting like because we made it, for them we've lost respect?

Danielle Savage

It is the slow death of Community and the slow death of Self, when we put all hopes and energies into the elusiveness of wealth. To be cool with it, I felt, is just a standard way of living. Never thought about the broken babies whose hearts need mending, never thought about the war and all the forgotten troops they're sending, never thought about the prison system and how many rules they are bending.

I couldn't keep pretending, when I finally realized the truth. I just hope that through this poem, this knowledge gets passed on to you.

Danielle Savage

Dear Woman

I am a woman. Weak vessel. Strong spirit. I am a woman, but from birth I've been taught that I should fear it. Muffle up your gentle nature. Water down the traits that show vulnerability the clearest.

So I became brash and reckless; taught to talk and rip through flesh with my words. Mind manipulatin' through beauty and curves; never really fit my personality. I felt uncomfortable doing it, but I settled in it and became quite well versed, actually.

"My body is my greatest asset; I don't want your time I want your wallet my dude, where the cash at?"

But oh woman, protect your heart, don't cast your pearls off to swine. Since a woman of noble character, who can one find? She is worth far more than rubies, precious diamonds and rare stones. Delicate as an Acacia flower because you know that a gentle tongue can break a bone.

Beauty should not come from outward adornment, gold jewelry, and fine clothes, but a gentle and quiet spirit, out of style that never goes. Tailored in decency and submission. Which is why society would see to it to make us compete and to scuffle.

Unstable, emotional wrecks and once again our mini queens are taught rivalry and the struggle; to come the cleanest, so I'm on YouTube beauty channels trying to step my contour game up. I played Barbie and Ken when I was a little girl so now my main focus is on how to get a man to choose up.

Insecurities plague the little girls inside all of us who just want to be loved. Who never got the affirmations they needed from their parents, because they were still growing up. So that little girl grew up with an unhealthy need for acceptance, constantly asking the question, "am I good enough"?

But I want to tell that little girl about the power inside, that you were skillfully created, you have a purpose so take pride. You will have roads bumpy, but you were born to manifest. Enjoy the ride.

Just don't ever forget to pay homage to the older woman, crowned with time and grace. And never look down on the younger woman, who you must assist so that she may be blossoming with hope and faith. Dear woman you are valuable, you are worthy, keep that in mind. Even though this is a weak vessel, this is a strong spirit, polish it and remember to shine.

Danielle Savage

Flustered

When you wanna do the right thing, but darkness seems to trail you. Freedom seems further than a life sentence bail you read The Scriptures, but to no avail. Frustrated with your own efforts. Who knew I couldn't do it by myself?

Who knew after the victory trials come back with a vengeance? Who knew I'd need Him every day; be asked to give up my independence if I'm really tryna live the life I claim to have on Sunday.

What a mundane sorrow to live with evil intentions. While I claim to know The King of Peace my close relationships are full of tensions.

But I'm supposed to be a witness to those I believe are lost, still they seem to have it together more than I do, throwing confusion on His name as I claim The Cross. Battled in my thoughts, flesh coupled with a sick mind, soaked in my desires, drowned, 'cause I'm only worried about getting mine. So, Selfish. So, God I need You to help me, I so want to live right, I so want to make You proud, I really wanna live a Holy life.

So tell me how to do it, how do I get power from above? Be completely humble and gentle; be patient, bearing with one another in love.

Do nothing out of selfish ambition or vain conceit. Sing, share, serve and to the younger generation we are

Danielle Savage

obligated to teach. Let the leader become like the servant and the greatest become like the child. Lord I'm nowhere near perfect, but for me no fame, my aim, is just to make You proud.

Danielle Savage

Forest Symphony

Like an autumn leaf, jazz swinging in the breeze, I am free; from the crown of my head to the sole of my feet. Pineal gland in tune, in sync with the trees, swaying, meanwhile the birds chirping, sweet sounds, let it be, let it be. Unfamiliar voices battling, big band style for the spotlight of it all; showy and crowy. Yet humble is the creek, still mighty is its call; steadying its chords, glistening toward its aim, splashing with life into solemn dry places, the bass, the rumble, flowing through my own veins. Swift black wings stroke against thick noon air, crisp as the blow of the trumpet; tough as the pat of the snare. Creating a sound that moves me; gentle, confident and sweet. Steady like that rhythmic bass line. Baby, I am free, I am free. So, let it be.

Danielle Savage

Human Nature

Imperfections are natural. We are a part of nature and nature is beautiful.

Still there is also a very real, unpleasant, ugly, sickening side of nature. It is quite opposite of the ascetically pleasing scenic visions that comes to mind when someone mentions a waterfall, cascading down into a babbling brook and meadow.

Nature isn't sanitized. It isn't deodorized. Untouched nature is not perfectly manicured or trimmed. It is raw, pure, and beautiful in all of its ways. Quite opposite of society's definition of paradise.

Nature is serene yes, but still so full of rage. Nature's scent is appealing and sometimes it's foul.

And we are all a part of nature like the rippling creek. And just like nature we are a fine balance of beauty and grotesque, delight and disgust, bliss and misery, delicateness and coarse.

Many sides to us all. And it could be called a crime, to expect us natural beings to just have one characteristic, one aspect, and one mode of being at all times.

We are the good and the bad. We are the highs and the lows. And that imperfect balance is what keeps us connected, connected to each other, connected to Self and connected to our Father, and connected to Mother Earth

BLYTHE DENNIS

Blythe Dennis is a singer, songwriter, and poet from Grambling, LA. She was born to Albert and Sarah Dennis and is the youngest of three children. From a very young age, Blythe showed an interest in the arts. She has been writing poetry and songs since she was an 11- year- old. Throughout high school and college, Blythe participated in a number of choirs and performing arts groups. She is also a member of Alpha Kappa Alpha Sorority, Inc.

In 2011, Blythe received her Bachelor of Science degree from Grambling State University. She is now a resident of Dallas, TX where she is currently pursuing her music. Blythe recently released her first EP entitled "The Heartbreak EP" which tells the story of young woman desperate to find love and the lessons she learns along the way.

Blythe Dennis

Fairytales

Ponies, princes, and princesses.
Glass slippers, pumpkin carriages, and wedding dresses.
None of these things mean much to me.
I resent ever reading fairytale books and ever believing
That a man would ride in on a white horse
And rescue me from a terrible fate
Or whisk me away from a burning building,
Ensuring my escape.
I HATE FAIRYTALES!
Who in the hell
Has ever seen a fairy?!
Why should I believe anything she has to say?
She is the reason
I go through this pain.
If it wasn't for her
I would know that I'm strong enough to save myself.
There would be no wishing on stars and throwing change into wells.
There would be no witches, warlocks, or a need to break spells.
If it weren't for her,
I wouldn't feel so bad every time that I fail.
I would know that there's no potion or incantation
That could grant me reprieve
And that the only way to succeed

Would be

To work hard and make blueprints out of my dreams.

Blythe Dennis

The Visitor

Today I had a visitor.
She looked awfully familiar
As if I was staring into life's mirror
Circa 2002.
I stared in amazement.
Such a beautiful face.
I wondered how she'd found me
For I wasn't in the same place.
Her eyes stung me like bees
As if she was displeased.
Yet they were calm
As if she knew my dreams.
"What happened to you?" she asked.
"You once had such high hopes."
I tried so hard to move but I felt as if my chair was bolted down
And my hands bound by ropes.
"What happened to your spirit? It once was so pure.
What did they do to you, my dear?
Was it too overwhelming to endure?"
I sat there transfixed.
Betwixt my mouth and my mind
The truth did reside
But I made it my mission to hide myself from myself.
"I know you well because, in you, I still dwell.
So regardless of if you decide to tell,

To exhale, to release yourself from this hell

Of your own creation,

I will still know.

Admit your transgressions

And retrieve your acceptance."

I felt wetness

Cascading from my eyes.

How could I have forgotten what I stood for?

How could I

Allow part of myself to die?

She looked at me like a neglected child.

I am older than she

Yet she was so wise.

"Remember that you are a prize.

Don't allow yourself to be victimized.

Let go of your foolish pride.

Remember the plans we made and the things we prophesied.

Please never deny me.

I am your creator.

It's you that I need.

You are the vessel.

Perform my good deeds."

KOURTNEY THURMOND

Kourt "Pastel Poet" Thurmond was raised in Mission Viejo, a small city just off the southern Californian coast. She graduated from Grambling State University in Fall 2014. She was a member of Lyrical Quest, Iota Sweetheart Inc., and GSU's TV Center. She is currently employed as a Pharmaceutical Sales Representative for Reckitt Benkiser.

Her hobbies include spending time with her nieces and nephew, novel reading, binge watching Anime, and learning/failing to cook. Some of the major things that inspire her are the walks of life of women around her and her Faith. She hopes by sharing glimpses of her own journey she can help other young women stand tall.

Kourtney Thurmond

I Collect Quotes

I collect quotes
I can write the perfect combination of words to express how I feel, I can recite them in my mind until they are engrained, bit when it comes to my mouth, I just can't find the sounds
So I collect quotes...
From people who know how not to leave their words unsaid
From people who do more then leave their mark on paper, rather than let the dream die in their beds
From people who spoke out loud,
Even quietly, while I shout in my head
These are the words of people who didn't find their voice;
their voice saved them instead

Kourtney Thurmond

Gumbo

She remembers the first time she tasted it
Rue brown like her Mother's eyes,
Bold spices of Zydeco lessons in the kitchen & laugher stewed over night;
The savory smell of her roots,
wafting through a Pepto-Bismal pink house
They tickled her taste buds and warm her soul

She watched her Mother added salt from a good days work, shrimp and mud bugs caught fresh by her Daddy's caring hands, Tabasco & bay leaves for that extra "umph" that only a Jones could keep up with

Back then She didn't realize how precious these moment were, or how memories can be held in recipes, how bonds can begin at kitchen counters, generation gaps can be filled with second helpings, how tables extend like family's, how joy can overflow beyond a life time if you have a big enough pot to hold it in…
And
How true it is that you are what you eat
She is all the flavors of her Mother
My Mom always said there's no gumbo like our Grandma's gumbo

Kourtney Thurmond

But what she meant was, there no love like her Mother's love.

Written May 10, 2014, as a Mother's Day gift to my mom, Kathy Thurmond.

Kourtney Thurmond

Herstorian

I am the daughter of dust and bones

Who's father sits upon a throne

I am a Godly likeness sculpted from dirt

And my mother is earth

I have been sitting on her rounded hips since birth

As she dances with the moon and around the sun

Bringing back gifts of melanin

Her heart is full of diamonds

And with the Nile she writes her name

I'm telling u this so you know from where my lineage came

I am the spoon full if brown sugar that helps the mediocre go down

Imported Koffee, brewed from the motherland

I am the caramel mocha antibiotic

My cocoa butter kisses are stronger then chronic

Breath in my aroma it's hypnotic

Sweet and smooth like Shea and coconut,

I'm your natural remedy and you can't get enough

African herbs and spices, oils and incense that entices you

To shake of the chains of negativity

Rejuvenate your memory

Restore your supremacy

And cure any false identity

Kourtney Thurmond

I am Mocha-hantas, Creol-patra

I was a king before a slave, and I'll D'jango any master

I am Afro-dite

Nappy headed creation of the Almighty

I am Nana Buluku, I am Yemaja, I am Oba, I am

Oshun,

Find her Proverbs or Ecclesiastes, that wise Woman

they speak of, I'm the one.

I am the chick that laid the egg,

I'm the Rib from which civilizations where bred

I am your muse

But you can call me WOMBman instead

Kourtney Thurmond

Even Mountains Cry

There's no such thing as a "hard rock" or a heart as cold as stone
Because even hills can moved, quietly they moan
Even frigid glaciers shed waterfalls
Tears of ice and snow

You'll find warm cores in violent volcanoes
And roaming rolling ranges, longing for a home

Underwater pools, in geysers, that have tried to suppress so much
Groaning cliff sides that breakdown, by the waters touch

Winding Canyons with rivers that are too deep for shallow pride
With every peak there is its valley where the wind carries it's sighs
Every mountain
Even Everest up high
Every single mountain
Is strong enough to cry

Kourtney Thurmond

Charred Steeples

Charred Steeples

Shattered stained glass

At the alter, smoke and ash

Wizards play God

Sheets on the pulpit

The 4 girls cry for the 9 saints

Old wounds re-slit

"A love that Forgives"

A pain re-lived

And all that remains

Is a cross inflamed

Kourtney Thurmond

Passive Aggressive Sub-Poem Number 7

You and I are too stubborn for love

Our walls have been built up too high

And our butterflies are too weak to flutter over

So, we throw love notes,

Wrapped around stones

Across the barrier

Hitting each other

But never making contact

Every missed message

Adds to the distance

The walls grow taller

The butterflies die.

Kourtney Thurmond

Flames of the Phoenix

Sometimes

The ashes She rises from

Belong to fires She started

Sometimes

They belong to fires

She LET burn

Kourtney Thurmond

Sleep Talks

I said your name in my sleep

The other night

It echoed in my head

Bounced around my ears

And woke me up

Not the startling sound of my voice in the silence

Calling out for someone who could not come or answer

Not the sudden realization that it was just a dream

No

It was your name

That woke me

Kourtney Thurmond

Prismatic Love (Excerpt)…

…Shine your light on me

I'll absorb your imperfections

Bounce off your reflection

Use some of your brilliant hues

And project them

So that I can glow back onto you

With all the glorious colors that you are

Together we'll illuminate the dark

LANDIS ANDERSON

Landis "Cyra" Anderson was born and raised in three out of five boroughs in New York. She developed into an artist at a young age. She began writing in elementary school, finding release journaling and writing poems outside of class assignments. During her adolescent years she gained a love for fine art as well as fiction writing, which led her to major in English and Studio Art in college.

In 2014, Cyra graduated from Grambling State University--where she gained experience in life and love, and began to discover and create herself as a person, woman, and artist. She draws inspiration from her personal life, people she's encountered, her environment, cultural and societal issues, as well as experiences of those close to her. As a painter, writer, part-time kitchen hair stylist, handy-woman and wood worker, budding graphic designer and photographer, night owl, avid reader, daydreamer, creator, Cancer(ian) just to name a few, she is Cyra.

Landis Anderson

Sisters

She is your Sister.

Uplift her

As though She were your blood.

Speak blessings over Her life

Empower and give peace

Honor and respect Her Femininity.

For Unity

Is a must.

Because She is your Sister,

And You are Hers.

Wipe clean those tears

Feed not Her fears.

For She has a right to be weak

In Her strength.

Be Her shade when the sun beats mercilessly,

Be Her laughter when the pain becomes too great,

Her guide when the world crumbles beneath Her feet.

And when She has everything,

Her dreams have been fulfilled

And Her cup overflows with the sweetest gold nectar

Smile and applaud,

Take a sip

And bask in the greatness that is She.

Because that is what Sisters do.

Landis Anderson

Lifted

Floating low but way more high

Time suspended for moments at a time

Life at ease

Cookies please

Drifting towards the sun and stars.

Warmth spreads like the wind

Welcoming and surprising

Laughter

Smiles

And joy Uprising

Harmony in my heart.

Pause and Go

Stop, rewind

Time is on repeat

I'm contemplating mistakes of life and love

Mind drifted deeply into the clouds above.

Landis Anderson

I Know A Man

I know a Man.
From ear to ear his name graces my lips as a smile.
Ambition unmatched, he is determined to earn that
which is already in his possession.
My heart,
Now his.
His perception is uncanny
Always in my head, speaking my thoughts aloud
As though they were his own.
I know a Man
Who courts my insecurities,
Wooing them past gates of confinement,
Guiding them to Queenly confidence.
I know a Man
Whose words elicit a dozen emotions at once.
Thrusting me into the depths of excitement and anxiety
While providing the greatest comfort I've ever known.
I know a Man,
Who knows my secrets and my flaws
Yet he loves me all the more.
His desire is to know my soul,
Protect my heart,
And align them with his.
I know a Man
Who wants to know all of Me.
My wants and needs

Landis Anderson

My passions and pain
So that he can give me everything I've lost and not yet found,
And show me who I am through his eyes.

Landis Anderson

I Don't Like Him

I don't like him.
But I think I want him.
I could list a dozen things about him that turn me off
But I want to kiss and taste him.
His demeanor draws me in
But his arrogance disgusts me.
Am I becoming a statistic?
I really don't like him.
I don't find him attractive
But I engage in this sexual banter
Ready for him to prove what he says is true.
Maybe it's the alcohol,
Maybe it's some hidden attraction
That I've just realized.
None the less I want him.
But I don't like him.
It's an aggravated attraction.
I want to slap him and then kiss him until his lips want nothing but me
Yet seeing him infuriates me.
What is this carnal effect he has on me?
Since day one
I've been victim to his appearance, his swag, his presence.
What is it about him?

Landis Anderson

His slick tongue angers me but makes me want to outdo him
Put him on his knees and worship me
Cherish what a grace it is to be before me
Admire me, want me.
I want him to want me.
The things I want to do, I could and would do
But, I don't like him.

Landis Anderson

Just the Tip

Slowly it eases its way in

Circling the outer rim

Sending chills running through me.

Slightly moist, the feel of it is familiar

But still it feels like it has been years.

I gasp in anticipation

It inches slowly inside, deeper.

Filling me instantly

Caressing each inner wall

Rubbing each one gently

Claiming its territory.

The need, tamed

The yearning, sated

Eyes roll back

Sigh of contentment escapes my lips.

How I've missed it

How numb I feel when it's within.

Time stops

Or slows

Or no longer exists;

All I know is this feeling

This ecstasy

Just the tip.

Q-Tip.

You Are to Me

Sometimes the things you do make me feel some type of way

But then I check myself

Gotta address myself

And remind myself

What your place is in my life

Who you are not and cannot be

Though part of me

Wishes things would be

Different.

Yet and still, they are not.

You are but a passing wind

A drifter trying to fit in

A sideshow attraction.

No, not the main event

Though you give off that pretense.

I must remember that you are not a permanent fixture

Never here to stay

No lingering there after

Gotta keep in mind

That no matter how much I wish you to be

There is a possibility

You might not even be akin to an interlude

A prelude to the temporary

Barely making memories

Just might be imaginary

When did things get so tricky?

Landis Anderson

The Rain

It comes and goes,

Much without warning.

The soft pitter-patter

Growing into a resounding symphony.

Its forceful presence

Emits a calm reverie

Bringing down upon the earth

Its cleansing and purifying waves.

Drip drop, plop,

again and again.

Washing away the worries of today

And the sins of yesterday.

Sporadically and righteously

Feeding the seeds of promised harvest,

Rinsing clean what once was of filth.

Leaving behind a pristine slate

And the hope of abundant tomorrows.

Landis Anderson

Different

And here I thought you were different.
Your tenacity was refreshing,
Attitude inspiring.
Even the assurance with which you spoke my name...it was different.
See, before I knew it I had fallen.
Dove head first, blindly
Into those deep brown orbs of yours,
The kind eyes that twinkle even in the daylight.
And that gleaming grin that makes me forget how to breathe sometimes,
Yet always causes my heart to
Thump-thump-pause for a few moments-thump-thump
in awe.
Pulse pattering wildly in my veins.
It was bliss.
We had a good thing you and I,
For the first time in ever I was me.
Unabashedly me.
As uncommon as it was, I stripped myself freely,
Trusting you without second thought.
Bearing parts of myself that others had not even glimpsed.
And yet I was left standing alone,
Naked for all the world to see and without a stitch of anything to maintain my innocence.

Landis Anderson

My broken pieces were exposed,
My fragility and imperfections reflected in those eyes I adored,
And I suddenly felt shamed.
Discarded and dismissed.
You took away the warmth that my cold heart had clung to,
The hope that you had once given.
And for a while I thought that you could and would be,
You were supposed to be,
My solace.
My get away from the frustrations of every day
My peace.
And I was supposed to be yours.
But apparently you aren't so different.

Landis Anderson

Ealy

You are golden.
Not merely in complexion
But in essence.
Your spirit shines through your eyes
And your smile,
Reflects the genuine heart of a child.
Though mild,
Our conversations flow freely
And intellectually
Leaving me satisfied yet craving more.
Your voice is like melted butter on homemade bread
Guttural and sultry.
And I don't even think you know
How it cloaks me.
Reminding me of comfort and peace
Strength and security,
Demanding the attention of the Woman in me.
In awe at the wonder of you, I am contentedly.
But beyond your physical attributes
Blessed as they are,
Your soul shines warm
Like sunlight through a glaze of honey.
I find myself drawn to it
To you,
Wanting to delve deeper than the ocean's floor
Into your mind

Landis Anderson

Ripe as a peach

And sweet as a plum.

You are an unexpected one.

A pleasure to behold

And I know,

That the worth of an man like you

Is priceless.

Even amongst a sea of rubies and gold.

Landis Anderson

My Best Friend

Her light is the sun

Its warmth radiates unintentionally

Her smile a celestial entity

Shining through the depths of eternity

In her heart resides enough care for the masses

Loving infinitely and irrevocably

Without expecting anything back and,

She inspires me to be greater than I could ever dream

I aspire to become at least half of the person she sees

My rock, my shoulder, a critic when I need it most

Aware of her beauty and brilliance but she is never one to boast

I doubt that she will ever know how much her friendship means to me

And freely

I give of me

Trust and loyalty

Love and support

To her

Unconditionally

REGERNIQUE RASCO

Regernique Rosco is a 2015 graduate of Grambling State University. She became a member of Delta Sigma Theta Sorority, Inc in 2014. In addition to writing and performing poetry, Regernique is a professional hairstylist. She has traveled to places like Paris, London, and Dubai.

Regernique Rasco

High

I am high; I am daily intoxicated, drunk and faded.
SOMEBODY GET HIGH WITH ME!
It was something thirsts quenching about him.
Something that the eyes of my soul never wanted to lose sight of,
I loved him.
He grabbed a hold and I never want him to let go, and believe me he never will.
Sometimes I do him so wrong, yet he still has the love and strength to hold on.
He is good to me.
He heals my spirit while satisfying my needs.
He truly comforts me.
HE gave us the BUGS, the BIRDS, the SKY, the SUN, this DAY, his SON and the TREES.
He is so kind to me.
Lord, I will love you forever and more.
SOMEBODY GET SPIRITCALLY HIGH WITH ME.
I am DRUNK, FADED, and INTOXICATED on LOVE, JOY, HOPE, HAPPINESS, HIS WORD, BLESSINGS, and PEACE.
Somebody find my scripture weed!
PUFF, READ, CONCEIVE THE WORD, HAVE FAITH, SHARE YOUR TESTIMONY, DON'T BE GREEDY, PASS IT TO ME and GET HIGH WITH ME.

Intoxicate your mind with something that will be nutritious to your SOUL.
Your spirit is screaming FEED ME, I'M HUNGRY.
MY RIBS are SHOWING.
They call me BONEY.
I haven't eaten in weeks.
You are giving into the cares of this world with God you should never FEAR, WANT, nor BE LONELY.
Where is the FAITH you claim to have on Sunday morning?
Your soul is mourning.
You barely have the strength or grip to hold on.
You Temple of Vision is blurry,
and you have just about forgotten God never lets go.
He always has his hand on you, no matter how far he lets you go.
Break into your Bible like you did those new shoes
and allow the words to penetrate your heart, which will light up the deeming flame in you that burns for God.
Take time out of this world to bury yourself in the book of good news.
Stay on your knees spiritually until they are BLISTERED, BURSED, and begin to BLEED.
Drown yourself in more than Psalm 23.
There is far more to the Bible and Christianity than the recycle scriptures we are accustomed to.

Regernique Rasco

So somebody light up that scripture weed, I'll pray for you, while you pray for me, lets share our testimonies and GET HIGH WITH ME.

Regernique Rasco

If Looks Could Kill

If looks could kill,
I would have been dead.
Closed Casket,
Due to an eyeball bullet shot straight through my head.
I looks could kill,
All the hateful words not needed said:
Such as "I HATE YOU", "DO NOT SPEAK TO ME" and
"I WISH YOU WHERE DEAD".
Rushing and running from a thirteen year old sweet tooth.
Oh we, oh my, if only my soul was bulletproof.
My pin beats my mind sometimes,
I write down things before I even think;
just how some people look at you crazy before they even speak.
Do not define me in your mind before you even get to know me.
The only reason you dislike me, is because you do not know me.
If looks could kill,
The coroner will be a very busy man,
pronouncing deaths dues to a dirty look, again and again.
I say if looks could kill just realizing the many ways they do.

That nigga pulled out his gat because of the way you looked at him,
and you pulled out yours because the way he looked back at you.
Now it's a shootout, and neither one of you are bulletproof.
That night two lives where took,
All over a got damn look, yah one may not be dead;
But he damn sure just been booked.
Look at me all you want,
take a real good look;
And I'll look back at you and crack a smile.
For those are the kind things I do.
I can care less about you mean mug,
That maybe the way your face looks.
The day I die and people ask, what was the cause of her death?
It damn sure will not be a LOOK,
If looks could kill
Just think of the many ways they do.
Please never allow a look to be the cause of death for you.

Regernique Rasco

Trayvon Martin

Why did I have to die today?
Why did a bullet have to meet me at an intersection?
I was only a block away from my destination.
A pack of Skittles and an Arizona were my only weapons.
Man, when did candy become so threatening?
Even though it was raining, maybe I should have never worn that hoodie.
I never imagined that my last supper would be a bag of candy.
Why not some of Granny's hot water cornbread and momma's greens?
Now I will never know who won the game, or if I won that bet I made with my brother,
But I thank God I walked to that store by myself.
Mr. Zimmerman, why did I have to be your victim?
Why did I have to be laid to rest before the final slam dunk?
Why did I have to take my last breath, NOT OLD and in a warm and cozy bed,
but in a backyard BY MYSELF?
From dust we come, to dust we go, I guess no one heard me when I cried and screamed for HELP,
But I guess that is just what I get, for traveling a little too far from the projects,
So YES MR. ZIMMERMAN, I guess I am in the wrong.

93 | So Lyrical, It Feels Spiritual

And I figure that is the reason you are still as free as my soul from my body.
Momma please don't weep,
Do not wish anything bad on this man,
 Because no matter what we are to love our enemies.
It had to be in God's Plan that I only lived to make it to seventeen,
So Daddy, hold on to my memories
For history can never be changed
No matter how hard you pray, wish you had a time machine, or that this was all a bad dream.
Post my last test on the refrigerator
Because I know I made an A or nothing less than a B.
Brother, please do not spend another night crying yourself to sleep.
For I will visit you all in your dreams, just how Papa used to visit me,
and remember, I am in the best place I could ever be...
LAID TO REST AND AT COMPLETE PEACE!

JA'MELL FAIRLEY

Ja'Mell Fairley was born and raised in Oakland, California. As a student at Grambling (2009-2014) she became a member of Sigma Alpha Iota Music Fraternity and studied Vocal Music Performance. Ja'Mell is now a graduate student at Fuller Theological Seminary and strives to inspire students and her community through the Word of God, music and culture.

Ja'Mell Fairley

Tell em Somethin'

You can tell the World I'm not afraid of the Gospel
Or, that I'm super saved
And the cross across my chest makes the enemy tremble by the very thought of it
Who needs a cape when you own wings like an eagle?
I'm a seed of Abraham reaping blessings not imagined by most people
Grace and mercy follows me temple
I'm skipping over traps the enemy has planned for me- lethal
You say that I'm boastful?
1 Corinthians 1:31
Now, I don't know everything
I just know that God Is my everything
And He gave up everything, so I may have everything
Including everlasting life, while you over there yellin' YOLO
And in case you didn't know
My God's a beast yo
He's the creator, He is YHWH
He is the Great I AM
He is Alpha and Omega
Sovereign, Omnipotent
He is everything, that I'm not
And because of that
I will forever give Him Praise,
I will forever lift up His name
You can tell the World that I am unashamed

Made in the USA
Middletown, DE
29 July 2017